Car Mechanic

ON THE JOB SERIES

Gate
HOUSE

On The Job: Car Mechanic
Copyright © Gatehouse Media Limited 2009
Photographs by Norman Butler
Edited by Catherine White

First published and distributed in 2009 by Gatehouse Media Limited

Printed by Wallace Printers, Westhoughton

ISBN: 978-1-84231-070-0

British Library Cataloguing-in-Publication Data:
A catalogue record for this book is available from the British Library

Gatehouse Media Limited provides an opportunity for writers to express their thoughts and feelings on aspects of their lives. The views expressed are not necessarily those of the publishers.

Editor's Note

Car Mechanic is based on an interview with James Counebear, a successful young mechanic from Rochdale, Greater Manchester. We should like to offer our sincere thanks to James for his generous contribution to this project and for being such a good role model for aspiring young engineers.

We should like to thank Pennine Honda, Rochdale for their assistance in giving us access to James at work. We should also like to extend our thanks to James's colleagues for their kind cooperation.

Car Mechanic is the first reader in the *On The Job* series which aims to help learners aged 14+ into work, into training and in their personal development. The series was devised by Vicky Duckworth, Senior Lecturer and Course Leader full-time PCET, Faculty of Education, Edge Hill University.

To support this publication, we have a range of tutor resources and student worksheets, available as en eBook on CD-Rom, which provides engaging and relevant material with embedded literacy and numeracy activities linked to the vocational interests and the functional skills needs of the student:

On The Job: Car Mechanic Tutor Resources
ISBN: 978-1-84231-071-7

My name is James. I'm 26 and I've been working as a car mechanic since I left school. My first job was at VW where I did my apprenticeship. I then transferred to SEAT for about a year before I moved to Honda. I've been at Honda now for about 3 years.

As a kid, I'd always been interested in cars and how they work and I really wanted to learn a bit more about them and get into the trade. I got my GCSEs at school - I had to have Maths and English at grade C or above - then I got my qualifications through college and my apprenticeship.

First I did NVQ levels 1 and 2 in Motor Vehicle Maintenance and Repair. I worked on day release at VW and, when they got to know me, they offered me an apprenticeship. I then did NVQ level 3 and the BTEC National Diploma in Motor Vehicle Studies.

I live about 8 miles from work and drive in every day. I start work at 8:30am and finish at 5:00pm. I get a 30 minute lunch break and two 15 minute breaks, one in the morning and one in the afternoon. I get paid for 8 hours a day, so it's a 40 hour week.

I wear a uniform – a black and red polo shirt and black trousers - and I always wear steel toe capped boots. Safety goggles are also provided depending on what you're doing, and also gloves if you're handling hazardous substances like refrigerant gas.

I report to Steve, the workshop controller, and then above Steve is Louise, the workshop manager. Steve is here all the time so he's the person I go and see if something's wrong. There are four technicians and Steve does the odd job too, if we're really busy.

Steve hands out the jobs each day. He tries to even them out fairly between us all, but we have different qualifications. Two of us have got Honda's diagnostic technician qualifications and two of us are normal technicians. My main tasks are service work and faults on the cars. I really enjoy the job. I just love learning new things about cars and how they work.

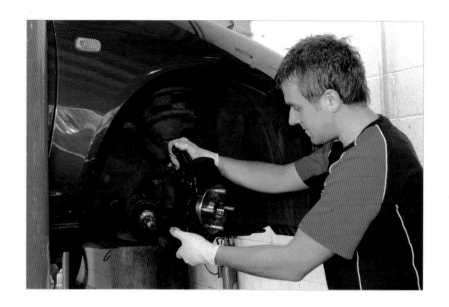

The pay is good as long as it's busy, because we get paid a bonus. We get our hourly rate no matter what and then, for every hour we can charge to the customer, we get extra.

There's a great atmosphere too. There's quite a bit of banter and football rivalry, of course. I support Manchester United, there's a Leeds fan and a few City fans. It's all good natured, but quite lively!

There's nothing I don't like about the job, except maybe getting dirty! There are a few awkward jobs but I just get on with them.

There's a bit of paperwork involved. You have job sheets that are given to you in a job pack with the car keys. If it's a service, you have to fill out a service sheet, a health check sheet and then stamp the service book.

We also have a timesheet to track our day and what we've done. We have to clock on and off jobs. Each job has a job number, so you just write in the start and finish times for the job and note down the parts you have fitted. The office add it all up at the end of the day and sort out the customer's bill. We're charged out at an hourly rate plus parts and then VAT on top.

I'm going to be put in for my Master Technician at the end of the year – there's only 28 in the country. I'll be doing a few courses before that too. Typically, you go on a 3 or 4 day residential when you're trained in things like electrics or air conditioning, for example. Afterwards you get a little booklet, like a passport, which shows what areas you're qualified in.

In 10 years' time, I'll probably still want to be doing what I'm doing now and then maybe aim towards management. At times I've thought about starting my own garage, but you just don't know what's going to happen with the economy. If I get to Master Tech, I'll be over the moon.

At the moment, I have some new lads working with me who want to get an apprenticeship with us. An apprenticeship is certainly something to aspire to. Like I said, I was with VW when I did mine - but they're all much the same. It's my role to encourage them and to show them the ropes.

We've got one lad coming in for work experience this week, one next week and one the week after that. Then we'll choose the best one out of the three to keep on. Two are from college and one left school and got a job in a garage, but you can't tell who's going to be good until you start working with them.

One of them could be stronger academically, but not as good with his hands. We're trying to get the best of both really. We like someone who's keen to do the work, who's always asking, "What can I do, what can I do now?"

When I left school, I didn't expect to get as far as I have done. I didn't think I'd be here now like this, but I'm proud of what I've achieved. My advice to anyone new is to stick with it and just keep your head down.

14

Keywords	
car mechanic	someone whose job is repairing the engines of vehicles
apprentice	someone who works for a skilled person for a period of time in order to learn that person's skills
apprenticeship	a period of time working as an apprentice
transfer	to move someone or something from one place to another
qualification	an official record showing that you have finished a training course or have the necessary skills
vehicle	a machine usually with wheels and an engine, which is used for transporting people or goods
maintenance	the work needed to keep something in good condition
repair	to put something that is damaged, broken or not working correctly, back into good condition
uniform	a set of clothes which has to be worn by the members of the same organisation or group of people
hazardous substances	dangerous materials
air conditioning	the cooling and dehumidification of indoor air
refrigerant gas	gas used in air conditioning systems
controller	a person who controls something
diagnostic technician	someone with the skills to determine the cause of a problem

Gatehouse Books®

Gatehouse Books are written for teenagers and adults who are developing their basic reading, writing or English language skills.

The *On The Job* series provides a range of readers and tutor resources with embedded literacy and numeracy activities linked to the vocational interests and the functional skills needs of the student. The series aims to help learners aged 14+ into work, into training and in their personal development.

Gatehouse Books are widely used within Adult Basic Education throughout the English-speaking world. They are also a valuable resource within the Prison Education Service, the Probation Service, social services departments and secondary schools - both in basic skills and in ESOL teaching situations.

Catalogue available

Gatehouse Media Limited
PO Box 965
Warrington
WA4 9DE

Tel/Fax: 01925 267778
E-mail: info@gatehousebooks.com
Website: www.gatehousebooks.com